Previous Works by
Patrick J. Cole

I Am Furious (Yellow)

Tangoed Up & Blue

NATURAL BEAUTY

AND OTHER POEMS

PATRICK J. COLE

Art by Barbara Merlotti

iUniverse books may be ordered through booksellers or by contacting:

iUniverse
1663 Liberty Drive
Bloomington, IN 47403
www.iuniverse.com
844-349-9409

Because of the dynamic nature of the Internet, any web addresses or links contained in this book may have changed since publication and may no longer be valid. The views expressed in this work are solely those of the author and do not necessarily reflect the views of the publisher, and the publisher hereby disclaims any responsibility for them.

Any people depicted in stock imagery provided by Getty Images are models, and such images are being used for illustrative purposes only. Certain stock imagery © Getty Images.

Art by Barbara Merlotti
https://barbara-merlotti.pixels.com

ISBN: 978-1-6632-3307-3 (sc)
ISBN: 978-1-6632-3308-0 (e)

Library of Congress Control Number: 2021924873

Print information available on the last page.

iUniverse rev. date: 12/07/2021

Love Questions

The answer to When is Now
The answer to How is Yes
The answer to What is Why
The answer to Who is You,
And Us.

I know, I know, less talk, more touch.

CONTENTS

WATER

FIRE

INTRODUCTION

F-bombs, sarcasm, groaning. Breath-holding, eye-rolling, tongue-biting, and moaning. The longer we live, the more grief and suffering accumulate. Somedays are especially difficult.

How we express ourselves when life presents another moment of frustration and disappointment is important. Embracing the pain before we release it can help.

Life is challenging; yet, it can also be joyful. Suffering and happiness inter-are.

Thank you for being here now.

May this book of poems help us find joy together.

EARTH

WHEN WE KNOW IT'S REAL

When we struggle for words
    To truly describe
The beauty of a peaceful moon;

When we're mesmerized
    By sunset or sunrise,
With no verbal way to express;

When joy warms our heart
    Or a breeze flows through us
Cooling our skin to the touch;

No notions are needed,
    Our body understands:
We are one with this time and this place.

WHO RESCUES WHO?

In one year's time, we have "rescued" five dogs
  Or, more accurately, they have rescued me.
They've taught or tried to teach me patience,
  As well as gratitude and humility.
Any failures were not on account of their teaching ability.

Who are they, who were they, what are their names?
  First, a spaniel, named Rosie.
Second, an island dog from St. Thomas.
  Third was Etta, a blind, deaf minpin-doxie,
And fourth, a nameless golden chow puppy.

Two of them came "knocking" on our back door;
  We brought them in, cleaned them up, had a vet check.
One we fostered until a family adopted,
  One we adopted until heavenly-trekked.
All were heart-touching, worth loving and divine respect.

We have four adopted rescues as part of our family;
  All four elders in their respective breed.
We are grateful to serve full- or part-time;
  Their presence reminds us of our interbeing creed;
Their love brings tears and confirms our mutual need.

MY FIRST REACTION

My first reaction is anger.
  I so easily take offense.
Chip on my shoulder forever,
  I find no joy in your nonsense.
Why am I so defensive?
  A relative's cruel grin?
"Come here, child. I won't hurt you."
  No! I won't be fooled again.
Or maybe karma is real;
  Must have really screwed up before.
My life is misery embodied;
  I promise, I won't do this anymore.
Help me, Rhonda or Sophia or Gaia,
  I need a break from this hell.
I thought life was meant to be happy,
  Not living in this deep, dark well.
I can't shake off this foreboding feeling:
  Is there worse coming 'round the bend?
Life seems like one long death sentence,
  From painful beginning to painful end.

WE STILL HAVE SOMETHING TO DO

Up and down, in and out, what will this day make?
    Many things repeat, maybe some things change;
Easier yesterday? Not so true today.
    Taking life as it comes? That's too hard to take.

Waking up once again; wrong side of the bed.
    Made your bed? Now lie in it? Can this be true?
Are we doomed to repeat 'til we recognize?
    Waking up simply means we are not yet dead.

Sometimes gay, sometimes not, sometimes we don't know;
    Feelings come. Feelings go. A cloud floats away.
Rise, my friend. Do report. There's work to be done.
    Clear your mind and perform 'til it's time to go.

ENJOYING THE SHOW

The nature guide placed the tarantula on my hand.
    It was as light as a butterfly.
Furry and soft, it crawled up my arm,
    Both beautiful and frightening, I will not lie.

Much earlier in life, at a scouting jamboree,
    I was stung by a large red hornet,
Hidden inside my shirt and likely
    Frightened as me; let's not forget.

Mother Earth, Mother Nature, Mother of Life,
    You all comfort, and you sting.
Sometimes you're a warm summer day;
    Sometimes a frightening stormy spring.

Sometimes a crisp golden autumn,
    Sometimes a harsh winter snow.
Cycles continue, each minute and hour;
    Let us make time to enjoy the show.

ONE TREE, ONE LONELY, FEBRUARY AFTERNOON

In the middle of a field, far apart from others, that lie in the woods
to the West,
Stands a tree, alone, exposed on every side; a tree looking
different from the rest.

How did this tree end up here, all alone? Does a tree ever have
a choice?
Perhaps our ancestral seeds blow where they will and all we have
is our voice,

To tell what we know, however small it may be, in whatever field
we find ourselves,
Sometimes what stands out, catches our eye, ends up on a mantle
or a shelf.

Alone and lonely are two separate states, but sometimes, they're
intertwined,
Like the branches of a tree, one lonely afternoon, in a late February
state of mind.

LIFE ISN'T ALWAYS PRETTY

Everyday there's a miracle of beauty somewhere ... if you look:
Big bright moon in the morning sky,
Dew on the morning grass,
Running water in the faucet,
Warm air from a heating vent.
So many beautiful things to see and feel
If you have eyes that can see, so it is said.

Thich Nhat Hanh reminds us, "No mud, no lotus."
Even feces can be seen for what they are,
Whether you can smell it or feel it or not.

The morning nurse greets us
Helps him to his feet, to his walker.
He slowly makes his way to the bathroom, where
After many minutes, he proclaims, "No bowel movement yet today."

But there, plain to see, is the deposit he left in the
Middle of his bed, which both
The nurse and I wordlessly agree,
"No mud, no lotus."
Healing occurs even if we cannot smell it or feel it or see it.

ONE LITTLE, TWO LITTLE

The poems and songs we grow up with
    Reveal the culture we are from,
Expose the perspective from which we see,
    Show how we're both smart and dumb,
Our geography, our history, our DNA,
    Wherever our journey may begin;
When we are fortunate, we will learn
    That no one will ever win.
Until everyone comes to realize,
    Until no one is left behind,
Until all life is treated respectfully,
    Then and only then will we find
Whatever I call you reveals my lack.
    Without you, I am blind.
With you, I can see more of Thee,
    True picture of our one mind.

TRAVELING WHILE I CAN

Moving often, as a child, I learned to love to leave:
    Every house, every school, with nothing up my sleeve.
With each move, I learned to cull and never to look back,
    With repetition, I acquired this hard-earned traveling knack:

First, travel lighter; not much space in a pillowcase,
    Learn to rank and rate and savor the few.
Second, there are always new people to be met;
    Down the road, there's always something new.

At first, I was sad to "lose" or "leave behind"
    My "friends," be they playmates or playthings.
Yet, I learned there were so many others to come;
    Impermanence is the song to sing.

And that is why I love to travel,
    Why brevity is a true friend.
For someday, sooner or later,
    I know my traveling days will end.

TREE HUGGER?

Advocate for the protection of woodlands
    Or a fool trying to save the world?
A crunchy, natural deodorant, faux hippie
    Or deep ecologist respecting all life?
Somewhere along this spectrum,
    Do you find yourself somedays?
Perhaps when "visiting nature"
    Or walking a sandy beach,
Picking up litter like you were taught
    By some conservation speech;
Or one more new green deal?
    Can we connect while grieving,
As our life ... slowly ... goes ... extinct?
    Will we someday find ourselves leaving,
Hugging a tree with our last breath?
    Or volunteer our organs
To a research body farm?
    What will it take to realize
We are born and die in Mother Earth's arms?

AFTER ALL IS SAID AND DONE

In the early morning hours, sometimes around the dusk
Even at noontime, if we dedicate the time,
Do we notice the softer sounds, ones so easily missed,
When we're otherwise busy or on the run?

It's during these times, we may hear our heartbeat
Or notice vibrations in our ears
Or feel the tingling in our hands and feet
And recognize how much is going on.

This is it! This is real! Noticing our breath,
Feeling our sitz bones, the position of our neck,
Acknowledging the gravity that allows us to be here,
Recognizing the earth from which we are born.

Without conscious effort, without deliberation,
This automatic flow of energy called "life,"
Whatever plans we may have or grand delusions arise
Our true home is here, after all is said and done.

NATURAL BEAUTY

Let me die in autumn, when green leaves turn to gold,
When red, orange, and yellow combine and then explode.
Let life pass in glory, a story to be told.
Let me die in autumn before I grow too old.

Worshipper of summer and winter is abhorred,
A woman of extremes, not one to be ignored.
True, she drives me crazy, but never am I bored;
Taught me what is holy and who should be adored.

And, so, on second thought ...

Let me die in springtime, when dead limbs bud anew,
Tulips break the surface and promises come true;
When love, like sap, will flow and every bird will coo.
Let me die in springtime and only die with you.

WIND

FREE RIDE

So far, breathing is free;
    I can inhale and exhale at ease
No oxygen mask needed,
    I can breathe as long as I please.
Without air, I would die quickly,
    Maybe fifteen minutes at most.
For many, it would be ten or less
    Without air ... we're a gasping ghost.

From our first to our last breath we live
    As beneficiaries of Mother Earth.
Her atmosphere provides us
    Lung power to enjoy with mirth.
I'm grateful for my life on this planet
    And the free oxygen it provides,
To live and grow and someday complete
    This adventurous free ride.

WHAT A BABY CAN TEACH US

Inside, outside, now I lay me down;
    Not for long, mind you; nothing lasts very long.
But for now, and maybe tomorrow, and maybe a week or month
after that,
    Noticing my breath I am grateful once again,
I can notice and appreciate your every little breath.

Regardless of the outcome or the income or any welcome at all,
    To sleep perchance to wake up—what more could I ask?
Merrily, merrily, or maybe not so merrily,
    We row our boats. Oh, what a delight it would be to dream—
Or even just to sleep the whole night through.

WE GO WITHOUT BREATH FOR ONLY SO LONG

Stumbling into enlightenment—heard that phrase before.
　　Must look it up and read it once again;
Truth is never once and done; repeatedly it calls.
　　We're ever drawn to the light, like I am to Zen.

We go without breath for only so long,
　　So too with water or food.
Our physical existence is dependent upon
　　Matter, both beautiful and crude.

Likewise, our spiritual life depends
　　Upon a love that flows free.
From one to another to others still
　　Truth lives in community.

PUT ON YOUR OWN OXYGEN MASK FIRST

✦

Life's been hard for a while now,
    Pandemic, aging, and other duress.
Her husband no longer cares for her,
    And her adult son cannot handle the stress.
Too tough, too messy, too hard, too old.
    No one wants her help or care.
Husband and son want out "right now!"
    They both want her out of their hair,
And, so, she cries, she worries, she frowns,
    And then she gives them what they want.
She finds another place to live,
    Her own crosstown apartment.
This wasn't how she hoped life would go
    This double-threat dose of strife,
But she practices smiling inside and out.
    She continues on with her life.
Maybe things will change in time,
    But right now, she needs to breathe.
She dons her smiling mask until
    Her smile is something to bequeath
To someone, anyone, if not the ones
    She originally intended her love,
For all life must continue on
    Until sunshine returns above,
Until someone returns her love.

LINGERING

I often rise an hour or more before my love,
    Who lingers in bed as long as she can.
She says she struggles to sleep at night,
    So I don't disturb her; at least, that's my plan.

The early morning time is whisperingly quiet,
    By nature and by my witness,
I rarely speak a word, which I enjoy,
    When my speech is little or less.

On some occasions, I mindfully attempt
    To speak as few words as possible
A whole morning or even a whole day,
    I find smiles become more visible.

Lingering in silence for as long as I can
    Helps me appreciate
My love, lingering in a warm morning bed,
    For as long as she can luxuriate.

MEANT TO BE BROKEN

It should come as no surprise
    That brokenhearted people
Come from broken promises
    And other broken pieces.

Physical or spiritual,
    We're broken in many ways;
Pieces of stained-glass windows,
    Composing a stunning frieze.

Once the sun shines through
    A prism reveals,
A creed of aspiration,
    A sky of disparate points.

Connecting the dots
    Helps to make sense of
The beauty still seen in
    Our very broken lives.

ONCE AGAIN

Can we separate the dancer from the dance?
     Can we know and be known?
Reciprocal motion is how we live;
     Breathing in and breathing out.
Embracing the dance is tasting the food
     Inside and outside of us.
What if there is no inner and outer?

     Only one, once again.

If we do not join the dance,
     If we do not dare to learn the steps,
Oh, what an impoverished life we will live,
     Missing out on a real embrace.

Let us sacrifice the known for the power to move
     More joyfully, more skillfully,
Conscious presence; the floor is our friend.
     We are balanced alone and together.

We are the dancer and the dance.
     We are the path; we are the Zen.

WATER

WE'RE OKAY, NOT TO WORRY, MY FRIEND

You have been with us six days without an accident.
    Your housebroken record had been perfect,
But today, you were interrupted and distracted,
    Knocked off schedule for the first time

I decided it was time for me to eliminate.
    I heard you waiting outside the bathroom door.
Then, as you walked away, I heard my wife exclaim,
    "Oh no, Shiba, not in the house."

You went on the hallway carpet;
    "A waterfall", my wife described.
"My fault," I say, and then to Shiba,
    "We're okay. Not to worry, my friend."

JUST ABOVE FREEZING

It's just above freezing outside
    Yet very warm where I now sit
In front of a large exposed window,
    Facing southward and fully sunlit.
The rays shine across my desktop
    And down across my lap.
My long-sleeved shirt and denim pants
    Too warm for the solar wrap.
Enveloping our rural homestead,
    Beating down on our exposed home
What little snow we have is melting.
    Perhaps all will be gone before the gloam.

MIDWINTER MELANCHOLY

Shakespeare reveled in midsummer,
    enjoying his Athenian romp
While humbly we survive midwinter
    With no circumstance or pomp.

No funny or cunning storyline,
    No hint of subterfuge,
Just a lonely cold winter's landscape,
    Neither miniature or grandly huge.

Missouri is a compromise
    Of pain and revelry,
The past too painful to forget,
    The future too vague to see.

Such is life in February,
    When we but hibernate.
Perhaps in spring, our joy will return,
    But now, we simply wait;
    Now, we listen and wait.

A MAN NEEDS AN EXIT

❖

Six inches of snow on a 300-foot driveway, and a shovel is my only tool.

The driveway connects to a gravel road, not yet or likely to be plowed.

My wife says, "Don't worry. It'll melt in a week; no need to leave the house anyhow."

I say "More snow on the way; rather shovel twice than have more to do tomorrow."

So, I go out, slow but sure, I shovel width and length. I'll shovel all day if I must.

You see, a man needs an exit, another way out, to avoid a slow death inside the house.

Call it cabin fever. Call it what you want. A man never wants to feel trapped.

By weather or by woman, it's important to have a path cleared well in advance.

So when she asks why I shovel when I could just wait, she knows the answer clear as day.

"Just to do it now, and maybe twice if I have to" is all I will say.

RENEWING OUR VOWS

Feel the dirt beneath our fingernails.
    The wet soil of spring gives us hope.
That winter will finally relinquish
    The hibernation we once needed.

But now, with glistening drops of rain,
    Fresh daffodils and blades of grass,
Say "Wake up." It's time to stretch again.
    It's time to bring forth new life.

We receive, continue, and touch the love
    That inspires each new moment.
Thank you, winter, for allowing us sleep,
    And, thank you, spring for waking us up.

Like each passing day and
    Each month's new moon,
Our planet's seasons refresh
    Our known and forgotten vows.

NOT SO FAR AWAY

A friend has discovered
    Or, more accurately, no longer denies
He has a serious problem
    With his weight, his heart, and his eyes.
Generous in so many ways
    To others all around,
He mistook self-compassion as
    Another serving, another round.
His doctor hoped a catherization
    Would be enough to start
A new health regime that
    Would restrengthen his heart.
But alas, no such luck.
    A heart bypass must take place;
If by chance, that should work,
    He will still be in the race.
For up to another decade
    Or maybe something less,
Better than a month or a week;
    Life can be such a mess.
Karma may not be instant,
    But consequences are sure;
Whatever the oral behavior,
    The heart must endure.

POETS AS LOVERS OF TRUTH

There are certainly times for pleasant sweet nothings,
  Cooing and wooing and sweet ear candies;
Love poetry, word music, is easily accompanied
  On guitar strings or bright piano keys.
"I love you. Do you love me? Oh, who cares? You're beautiful.
  The world seems perfect in your company.
Nothing else is as important to me
  Than our hearts beating happily."

But, let's get real. Life's not always a picnic.
  And even picnics have their share of troubles.
There are ants and rain and forgotten items
  And singles wishing to be doubles.
More seriously still, there's challenges a many.
  No peace or justice and real-life oppression.
If we're true to ourselves, we must admit
  No one can be a single possession.
So, poets take note—there's work to be done;
  Let truth ring out on the page.
If we have an ear; let's speak the whole truth.
  Poets as prophets can remake this age.

LADY JULIAN SAYS IT'S ALL LOVE REVEALED

Before we were born,
　　Before the universe even,
When only love existed,
　　Events began, action was taken,
Love was revealed.
　　If Dharma is truth,
Then Dharma is love, and
　　Dharma is love in action.
There is thought, there is speech,
　　And then there is action ... behavior ... what we do.

I do not know another's thought.
　　I may or may not hear you speak,
But I see your behavior; I see what you do.
　　Someone said believe half of what you see
And nothing of what you hear.
　　Someone said, be careful of your thoughts,
Because they will lead to speech, and
　　Be careful of your speech, for it will lead to action.
Careful, careful, careful, but
　　I can only believe your action.

SILENCE IS GOLDEN

Is speech silver, or is it cheap?
    Regardless, silence is golden.
Better to say nothing at all
    Than to be left holding
The resentment, the anger,
    The misery and pain
Of someone offended
    By your misguided aim,
To shed some wisdom,
    However well-formed;
To shed some light
    Where darkness swarmed:
A poor conversation,
    A waste of air space;
Better to say nothing
    Than add to the race
To the bottom of sense,
    The basement of hell,
Where no grace is given
    Or patience will dwell.
So keep your silver,
    Thirty pieces ill-gotten.
I'll keep my mouth shut, and
    Nothing need be forgotten.

FIRE

FOCUS

Focus, focus; what are we really looking at?
    Is it this? Is it that?
What causes and conditions are present?
    What message is being sent?
To entertain, to educate, to inspire,
    To provoke, to activate, to set afire?
To be a court's jester or kingdom prelate,
    A person of means, another rich ingrate;
A consigliere, forecaster, or confidant,
    A clerk, docent, or whatever you want?

Are you sure? Am I sure? Do any of us need to be sure?
    Surely, our motives are not entirely pure.
I'm a writer, I'm a poet, I'm a messenger of some sort.
    May we learn ... how to discern ... or if it's time to abort.

DIE. ZOMBIE. DIE.

Lifeless, apathetic, completely unresponsive,
    Just waiting for our next dose
Of whatever it takes to reanimate;
Shit cleanup is a job we inherit, doubtfully one we chose.

In a universe not always beautiful,
    From death to death with incessant pain—
God, this truly sucks; you must really hate comedians
Are compassion and wisdom the aim?

When everything is snafu,
    What a groovy consolation prize.
Designed for obsolescence …
Everything impermanent; now, that's a pleasant surprise

The quicker we die the less pain we endure?
    With no wasteful sentiment
Let's clean up some shit and die, zombie, die.
May the Pure Land be our next settlement.

WHEN OUTCOME DOESN'T MATCH EXPECTATION

❖

Supposedly our paths are not that unique.
    Nature and nurture combine
To produce predictability
    Amidst the maddening horde.
Every result makes perfect sense
    When looking back over time.

And yet, let us ...

Set some goals, do some tasks,
    Hopefully do good along the way.
    Hopefully better if not perfect,
    Hopefully friendship if not results,
    We will acknowledge on our final day.

WE NEED A CHANGE OF VIEW

We need a change of view, not just sight but heart too.
The snow has fully melted, and spring cleaning comes to mind.
So many things to do, so many things to undo.

Mend the fences, pick up branches, groom the trails. What are the chances
That all of this will be delayed once we find
More urgent repairs are needed once the puddles have receded?

We need a change of view.
Looks like spring will more than do.

SUNRISE BEFORE THE SUN APPEARS

Slowly, the black sky turns blue and the bare winter trees reveal
their emptiness;
From this direction, I cannot yet see the sun but know it's there
nonetheless.
I've lived for more than sixty years and seen many sunrises in
my life;
Each mark a new beginning: today brings fresh yeast and fresh
strife.

Are we a cocreator, fashioning our own matrix mind?
Is the cosmos a blank page inviting each artist to design,
Whatever near future desired, whatever near past left behind?
Do sixty-some years expand or restrict? Can we resurrect, or
must we resign?

But now, the blue sky grows brighter, and feathery white clouds
materialize,
Orange and yellow highlights announce that soon the full sun will
arise;
And now, our mood grows brighter, reflecting the nature we see;
Here and now is oh, so pleasant; with no past or future, we are
free.

TWO OF THE 84,000 DHARMA DOORS

Some say there are 84,000 doors to the truth, so find your own
and be set free,
    Become your own teacher, be your own lamp, live your own
    truth.
There are things that others can share, but
    None of it means anything until you make it your own.

Liberate yourself, and maybe someday you can share too
    If someone should ask.
The best teacher is the one who lives their truth
    And dares to live life without a mask.

What works most effectively, for them,
    To reduce suffering and be happy in this life.
Seek this kind of teacher, and better yet,
    Become this kind of teacher, for yourself
        And any others who may someday ask:
            How do you know what you know?

WHAT WE ARE LENT

Sometimes, we think too much,
    Sometimes not enough;
Sometimes it's time to pause and breathe;
    I think that's the "right stuff."

Or is it right view, right action,
    Or right effort?
Whatever it is,
    Let's recognize the common hurt,

Then embrace and smile
    And enjoy this moment.
It's a short ride, after all,
    And life is what we are lent.

FILLING THE GAP

Two plus two equals ten; of course, we all know that.
Some information here, some from there.
Then, a whole story derived from just a chat
You love me; no, you hate me; or is it fear and not love at all?

It's as plain as the nose on our face, isn't it?
Or, are there some "facts" we're choosing not to recall?
How can we be sure what is true or not?
Are we ever sure of the "truth"?

In the meantime, I love you is the only moment we've got.
Here and now, not back then or some future hence.
Right now, I love you,
Even if it's only mere coincidence.

WE ARE INVINCIBLE (NOT)!

Was it yesterday or decades ago
    That we felt so confident,
That anything we chose to do
    Became an accomplishment,
Anything was possible,
    Anything at all.
Just focus and initiate,
    Then bust through one more wall.

But the walls seem to multiply
    And the energy needed as well.
Best to let some others join
    In this common march through hell.
May be time to change our perspective.
    Let the challenges be.
Time to be grateful for
    Our tiny slice of eternity,
Not as strong as we used to be.
    Our body has changed a lot.
When we awake, we'll realize,
    We are invincible (not)!

A FRIEND'S LIFE MATTERS

He asked me if I thought he'd make it:
    Survive his surgery
"Yes, I do," I replied, clear and plain,
    "There's still a lot for you to do."
He said he wasn't afraid to die
    And agreed that much remained undone.
He showed me his office filled with papers,
    Talked about requests for his archives,
Recalled his written yet unpublished work,
    His thoughts for more to write,
Talked about his son's wedding to come,
    Looked forward to a granddaughter's visit that night.
His garden needed tending.
    He could get back in shape easily
If he could only breathe easier.
    It wasn't asthma, after all, you see,
But the need for a surgery (or two).
    He wasn't afraid to die,
And there was still plenty to do beforehand.
    His life still mattered—that's why.

WHAT IS TRUTH?

Your truth, my truth. Does anyone own the truth?
    Your god, my god. How many gods do we need?
To care for those who need care;
    To heal those who are sick;
To feed those who are hungry;
    How many gods do we need?
I know that thunder and lightning are scary.
    I know I didn't make myself.
I know somedays its hot and dry
    And other days wet and cold.
But I also know that when we are kind,
    When we look out for each other,
Our lives are easier and happier,
    Our smiles tell me that is true.
So spin some stories, if you like,
    About the hunter in the sky,
The big and little dipper,
    Sending comfort to all that cry.
But let's not argue over gods;
    Let's not fight over truth
Instead, let's share blankets,
    Clean water, and healthy food.

WE DON'T NEED GREED

There are many things we need,
Like air and water and twelve hundred calories a day,
Some basic clothing and shelter
To keep the cold and hunger away,
Some mental stimulation,
Perhaps a spiritual connection,
Some sense of where we are
And a reasonable direction.
Maintain some equilibrium.
Obtain some quality feed;
Otherwise, not much else,
And we sure don't need greed.
Intense or selfish desire
for wealth, power, or food
Won't do us any favors,
Won't produce any good.
The sooner we understand this,
The sooner we realize
The truth of our existence comes
From letting go of our lies.

THE LITTLE RED HEN TAUGHT ME HOW TO GO ALONE

When presented with a puzzle, I begin to assemble;
　　Presented with a problem, it's something I must solve;
Presented with a question, I feel compelled to answer;
　　I just assume the challenge is mine to resolve.

Over time, I have learned there are process goals too,
　　But again, I'm compelled to process on my own.
When others say they're available but don't show up or pull their weight
　　I don't wait or deliberate, nor whine or groan.

I plow on, thinking harvest time is very, very near.
　　Best to do something before the day is gone.
Maybe my effort will be an example somehow, or maybe,
　　Like the Little Red Hen, I will sadly eat alone.

You see, everyone wants more,
　　But not everyone wants to work.
So let it be written and let it be done:
　　Reap your own harvest and don't be a jerk.

CHOOSING OUR PROJECTION

We cannot help projecting
    Whatever we have inside,
Poker face withstanding,
    Our hearts reveal our tide
Are we high or low?
    Are we healthy here and now?
Try as we might, we cannot disguise
    The symphony on our brow.
Are we loving or hate-filled?
    Are we kind or mean?
Our feelings exude and reveal;
    Our inner world is seen.
And so I pay less attention
    To my looking glass,
More attention to what we see
    And avoid my being crass
As the moon reflects the sun,
    As water reflects the moon.
My goal is to clearly project
    The truth of bright high noon.

PLAN A, PLAN B, PLAN C

It's said that life is what happens while we're making other plans,
    Yet some of us were born to plan,
And with training, we learn to make more than one;
    We are taught to make backup plans.

Why so many plans when life surprises?
    Why be prepared for any contingency?
When there's so little we can control, is it possible
    To remain calm amidst emergency?

Oh, help us be the peace to support others.
    Help us be a way station in each storm.
May we reveal the wisdom that supports us,
    May we reflect the sun that keeps us warm.

YESTERDAY

Yesterday was the anniversary of my father's death;
    He died thirteen years ago.
I've thought of him often this month but not yesterday.
    What about yesterday don't I know?

My father was the last of eleven children;
    Called Jack though his name was John.
My father claimed he had a chip on his shoulder,
    Seemed proud that he kept it on.

A boxer, a carpenter, a joker to the end,
    Always with a twinkle in his eye.
Absent from my life most of my life,
    But at least we said goodbye.
    At least we said goodbye.

HOW I COUNT TO ZEN—43

With Ch'an, I better understand
    Myself, my mission in time and space.
No drama and dharma are what I seek;
    Decent and solid is my true face.
When change is where we live,
    From dhyana to zazen I count,
At least to five; breath to body
    To kindness, twelve links and paramount.
The flower tells me no fixed formula
    To finding a peaceful moon,
Observer and observed, no mind.
    Full, half, Burmese, or kneeling rune
Lying down or walking; all are healing,
    Breathing from belly my half-smile arises;
I hear One Love in every sone.
    Zazen, kinhin, and chanting surprises
Plan, do, check, act through all my days,
    Kaizen by point or by the whole.
I ask why at least five times,
    To comfort any painful earhole,
To love thee with smiles and tears and breath.
    I fondly count till my counting ends
And love Thee better through birth and death.

(With a nod to Elizabeth Barrett Browning's "Sonnet 43")

WHICH VERSION WILL WIN TODAY?

Enough about the need for hard work.
    I'm tired of all these excuses.
You say to receive the best requires
    My effort to the point of bruises.
I thought my winning smile was sufficient,
    Maybe with a twirl and a curtsy.
But no, you say there's practice and drills
    To the point that everything hurts me.
Why must there be pain before elation?
    Why must there be so much work?
All I want is joy that comes easy,
    No pushups, just an easy twerk.
Why must there be blood, sweat, and tears?
    Is success some sadistic sewn reap?
I'd rather it be fun, light, and breezy,
    Like a gleeful diving board leap.
You say I can play all I want
    But rewards go only to the brave
Who put in the time and the energy
    That releases the creation we crave.
So now, I must decide, once again,
    How do I want to proceed,
With focus and clarity and drive
    Or more ignorance, hate, and greed?

AFTERWORD

Energy never dies; it is redistributed. Our human body is composed of energy, electrical and chemical, that generates and activates the cells that make up our composition.[1]

Our body has approximately 30 trillion human cells, of which 300 million die every minute. In addition, the body also contains approximately 38 trillion bacterial cells, most of which reside and work in our digestive tract. Our body contains more nonhuman cells than human cells. Some might say we exist as a host for other lifeforms.

There are some 200 different types of human cells in our body. The largest number being red blood cells which live for about 120 days. The average body makes about 2.5 million red blood cells every second or some 225 billion red blood cells per day. In contrast, white blood cells live for only thirteen days, a skin cell lasts approximately four weeks, liver cells live up to eighteen months, and finally, brain cells may stay alive throughout a person's life.[2]

Finally, we can come to enjoy the beauty and brevity of each cell, the preciousness of the earth, air, water and fire that provide for the creation and sustenance of our oh, so brief lives. We have much to be grateful for on this planet.

---

[1] Death Physics: What Happens to Our Energy When We Die? | Futurism
[2] How Many Cells Are in the Human Body? Types, Production, Loss, More (healthline.com)

Aware of our good fortune, may we be brave, truthful and unselfish. May we be decent. May we be kind and smile often. Come, let us find joy together.

With gratitude, Patrick Cole

ACKNOWLEDGEMENTS

There are many who have directly or indirectly contributed to this work.

- First, I am grateful to my partner, Linda, who inspires my work and to her sister, Barbara, who illustrated this and two previous books. Their perspective on the world reveals beauty I would have easily missed without them.

- Next, come parents and ancestors, family by blood and by marriage, and children and grandchildren. Our interbeing is both surprising, comforting and continually educational.

- Many thanks to my early preview readers, who provided reactions and suggestions; especially those who agreed to be mentioned here: Ari Bouse, Katie Bradley, Melanie Chen Cole, Ben Cole, Kim Cole, Ronald Macfarlane, Mary Ann Markowicz, Dave Wilson, and Oliver Wirths. Their willingness to sift through a ragged early draft helped me identify some wheat from the chaff.

- Finally, I acknowledge the poets who have most influenced me: Maya Angelou, Elizabeth Barrett Browning, Billy Collins, Emily Dickinson, Bob Dylan, T. S. Eliot, Robert Frost, Mark Nepo, Mary Oliver, Tom Wayman and David Whyte. Please note that none of them are aware of my work; however, their work has brought inspiration and joy to my own.

For all of those mentioned above, I am sincerely grateful.

Printed in the United States
by Baker & Taylor Publisher Services